ACCESS TO ENGLISH

STARTING OUT

WORKBOOK B

MICHAEL COLES and **BASIL LORD**

Illustrated by Ivan Ripley

D1232801

OXFORD UNIVERSITY PRESS

Oxford University Press. Walton Street, Oxford OX2 6DP
OXFORD LONDON GLASGOW
NEW YORK TORONTO MELBOURNE WELLINGTON
KUALA LUMPUR SINGAPORE JAKARTA HONG KONG TOKYO
DELHI BOMBAY CALCUTTA MADRAS KARACHI
NAIROBI DAR ES SALAAM CAPE TOWN

© Oxford University Press 1977
First published 1977
Fourth impression 1979

ISBN 0 19 453716 1

Set in Monophoto Times by
Tradespools Ltd, Frome, Somerset
Printed in Hong Kong by
Yuen Fung Printing Co.

CONTENTS

Summary 11   3
Summary 12   8
Summary 13   13
Summary 14   18
Summary 15   23
Summary 16   27
Summary 17   30
Summary 18   36
Summary 19   40
Summary 20   44
Key to Pronunciation   *Back cover*

Summary 11 Language Summary

1. PRESENT PERFECT

Go to the window and say:
  I'm going to the window.
Open the window and say:
  I'm opening the window.
Go back to your chair and say:
  I've opened the window.
'I've opened the window' is an example of the Present Perfect Tense. 'Opened' is the Past Participle of the regular verb 'open'.

Say and write the Past Participles of these regular verbs:

ask	examine . . . .
arrive	recognize . . . .
look	play . . . .

Now say and write the Past Participles of these irregular verbs (you can find them on pages 143–4 of your book):

see	go	do . . . .
write	put	be . . . .
drive	get	make . . . .
say	have	break . . . .

We use this tense for past actions whose time is not given and for actions in an unfinished period of time.

a) Affirmative

Say the sentences in Table 1. Read the sentences in Table 2.

1)

I've You've We've They've	had breakfast. smoked a cigarette. tidied the house. read the newspaper.
He's She's	written a letter.

2)

I You We They	have	had breakfast. smoked a cigarette. tidied the house. read the newspaper.
He She	has	written a letter.

We often use the word JUST with this tense.
Say and write what Arthur has just done in these pictures:

a) . . . . out of bed.

b) . . . . a shave.

c) . . . . out of the house.

3

d) .... a newspaper.

e) .... on the bus.

f) .... at the library.

b) **Interrogative and Short answers**

Ask and answer these questions:

Have	I you we they	had breakfast? smoked a cigarette? tidied the house? read the newspaper? written a letter?
Has	he she	

Yes,	I you we they	have.
	he she	has.

No,	I you we they	haven't.
	he she	hasn't.

Look at this list of phrases:
started Chapter 12?
read all this book?
had lunch/dinner?
done your homework?
been to the cinema this week?
seen Richard Burton's new film?
Now practise this dialogue with a friend, using the phrases from the list.
Have you started Chapter 12?
    No, I haven't/ Yes, I have. Have you?
No, I haven't/Yes, I have.

c) **Negative**

Say the sentences in Table 1. Read the sentences in Table 2.

1)

I You We They	haven't	had breakfast. smoked a cigarette. tidied the house. read the newspaper. written a letter.
He She	hasn't	

2)

I You We They	have	not	had breakfast. smoked a cigarette. tidied the house. read the newspaper. written a letter.
He She	has		

Look at the pictures on pp. 3–4 again and say and write what Arthur has done and hasn't done.

a) .... out of bed, but........................ his

clothes on.

b) .... a shave, but .... a bath.

c) .... out of the house, but .... the

door.

d) .... a newspaper, but...................... his

change.

e) .... on the bus, but .... his fare.

f) .... at the library, but .... through

the door.

It's late in the evening. You haven't rung your friend Jim, but you are too tired to do it now. You say:

Oh dear! I haven't rung Jim.

There are many other things you haven't done today. Say the same sentence for these things:

a) (WRITE) to Aunt Joan   c) (TAKE) my medicine   e) (DO) my homework

b) (BUY) a new pen   d) (WASH) the car   f) (BE) to the bank

2. DO THE -ING

Learn these phrases:

Mrs Newton	has done is doing is going to do	the	shopping. washing up. ironing. cleaning. sweeping. cooking. gardening.

3. HAVE A . . .

Learn these phrases too:

Arthur	has had is having is going to have	a	sleep. shave. wash. shower. bath. meal. drink. smoke.

4. Idioms with CHURCH, HOSPITAL, SCHOOL, BED

These words are used without the definite article in some expressions.

be	at	church school
	in	hospital bed

go	to	church school hospital bed

If you are there or are going there for the recognized purpose of the place, no article is needed. If you are visiting, the article is needed.

Put IN, AT *or* TO *in these sentences. Also put* THE *if necessary.*

a) Arthur never goes ...... church. He usually stays ...... bed late on Sunday morning.

b) Mary has gone ...... hospital. She wants to see Bruce.

c) Where are the children? They're ...... school. Where's their mother? She's gone .... school too. She wants to speak to the teacher.

d) The ambulance has taken Bruce ...... hospital. Dr Newton is going to go ...... hospital tomorrow to see him.

e) Where are the Newtons? They're ...... church.

f) Where's Sheila? She's gone ...... bed.

g) This is a pretty village. You've visited the pub, but have you been .... church?

5. BOTH; ALL; NEITHER; NONE

There are three patterns with BOTH:

> **Both** Arthur and Mary live in Middleford.
> They **both** work at the library.
> **Both** of them are young.

There are three patterns with ALL:

> **All** the guests have gone home.
> They have **all** said goodbye.
> **All** of them are tired.

There are two patterns with NEITHER:

> **Neither** Sheila **nor** Mary can sit down.
> **Neither** of them has a drink.

There is only one pattern with NONE:

> **None** of the seats are free.

Answer these questions with BOTH OF THEM, ALL OF THEM, NEITHER OF THEM, *or* NONE OF THEM:

a) Which is married—Arthur or Bruce? ....

b) Who lives in Applefield—Bruce, Mary or Mrs Harrison ....

c) Which of the two girls likes parties—Sheila or Jennifer? ....

d) Who works at the library—Mary, Arthur or Mr Steele? ....

e) Which book is in the library?—*King Arthur* or *A New History of Middleford?* ....

....

f) Which is Arthur's sister—Mary or Sheila? ....

g) Who lives in Middleford—Mr Steele, Mrs Harrison or Sheila? ....
....

h) Who works in London—Arthur, Dr Newton or Mr Steele? ....
....

Vocabulary

arrive	ə'raiv	....	lorry	'lɔri	....
ask	ɑːsk	....	meet	miːt	....
bar	bɑː*	....	move	muːv	....
bath	bɑːθ	....	neither	!naiðə*	....
bit (n.)	bit	....	news	njuːz	....
bitter	'bitə*	....	none	nʌn	....
both	bouθ	....	nor	nɔː*	....
break	breik	....	oven	'ʌvn	....
breakdown	'breikdaun	....	patient	'peiʃənt	....
certificate	sə'tifikət	....	recognize	'rekəgnaiz	....
clean	kliːn	....	sad	sæd	....
cottage	'kɔtidʒ	....	shave	ʃeiv	....
couple	'kʌpl	....	sherry	'ʃeri	....
dirty	'dəːti	....	shower	'ʃauə*	....
even	'iːvn	....	shut	ʃʌt	....
finish	'finiʃ	....	start	stɑːt	....
garage	'gærɑːdʒ	....	sweeping	'swiːpiŋ	....
insurance	in'ʃuərəns	....	tidy (v.)	'taidi	....
ironing	'aiəniŋ	....	tomato	tə'mɑːtou	....
juice	dʒuːs	....	wait	weit	....
last	lɑːst	....	world	wəːld	....
lend	lend	....			

Casanova	ˌkæsə'nouvə

Summary 12   Language Summary

1. HOW LONG?; FOR; SINCE

> I'm a student.
> The Newtons know the Lesters.
> We live in Middleford.
>
> Mrs Harrison has a cat.
> Arthur works in the library.
> Bruce is in hospital.

How long	have	you been a student? they known the Lesters? you lived in Middleford?	I've been a student They've known the Lesters We've lived in Middleford	for	six years. a month. three weeks.
	has	she had a cat? he worked in the library? he been in hospital?	She's had a cat He's worked in the library He's been in hospital	since	1972. January. last month.

Notice that we use the Present Perfect Tense in HOW LONG questions and answers. *Complete these sentences, as in the example:*

'Arthur lives in Middleford.' *'How long has he lived there?'*

a) 'Mary works at the library.' 'How long . . . . ?'

b) 'Bruce has a fast car.' 'How long . . . . ?'

c) 'Dr Newton works at Applefield Hospital.' 'How long . . . .

. . . . ?'

d) 'Mr Lester is an engineer.' 'How long. . . . .

. . . . ?'

e) 'Mrs Newton has a small dog.' 'How long . . . . ?'

f) 'Arthur knows Sheila.' 'How long . . . . ?'

Notice also that we use FOR with a period of time and SINCE with a point of time. *Put FOR or SINCE in front of these phrases:*

a) . . . . : ten days   e) . . . . three weeks

b) . . . . last week   f) 1974

c) . . . . Tuesday   g) . . . . last Saturday

d) . . . . five minutes   h) . . . . many years

Practise these dialogues with a friend:

a) Where do you live?
   In . . . .
   How long have you lived there?
   For . . . ./Since . . . .

b) What's your job?
   I'm a . . . .
   How long have you been a . . . .?
   For . . . ./Since . . . .

Hello! I haven't seen you for several weeks.
I'm hungry. I haven't eaten anything since breakfast.
Bruce is in hospital. He hasn't been to work for three days.

Now say and write two sentences about these pictures, as in the example.

FOUR DAYS

The kitchen is dirty. Mrs Harrison hasn't cleaned it for four days.

SUNDAY

a) The television is ....

....

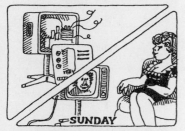

CINEMA   CLOSED

TWO MONTHS

b) The cinema is ....

....

LAST FRIDAY

c) Arthur has ....

....

THREE DAYS

d) Bruce is ....

....

9

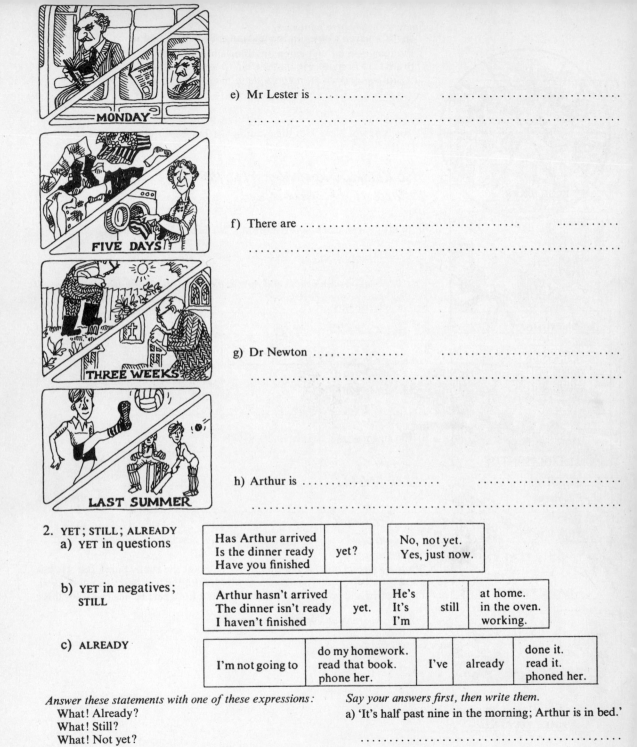

e) Mr Lester is ....

....

f) There are ....

....

g) Dr Newton ....

....

h) Arthur is ....

....

2. YET; STILL; ALREADY

a) YET in questions

Has Arthur arrived		No, not yet.
Is the dinner ready	yet?	Yes, just now.
Have you finished		

b) YET in negatives; STILL

Arthur hasn't arrived		He's		at home.
The dinner isn't ready	yet.	It's	still	in the oven.
I haven't finished		I'm		working.

c) ALREADY

I'm not going to	do my homework.	I've	already	done it.
	read that book.			read it.
	phone her.			phoned her.

Answer these statements with one of these expressions:
   What! Already?
   What! Still?
   What! Not yet?

Say your answers first, then write them.
a) 'It's half past nine in the morning; Arthur is in bed.'

   ....

b) 'It's eleven o'clock in the morning; Sheila has had lunch.'

. . . .

c) 'It's four o'clock in the afternoon; Mary has gone home.'

. . . .

d) 'It's eight o'clock in the evening; Arthur hasn't finished work.'

. . . .

e) 'It's eleven o'clock in the evening; Mrs Harrison is cooking dinner.'

. . . .

f) 'It's two o'clock in the morning; Mr Steele hasn't gone to bed.'

. . . .

Study the information in this table and then write the same information about yourself and a friend in the two empty columns.

		John White	Jack Lester	You	Your Friend
1.	Name	John White	Jack Lester	You	Your Friend
2.	Age	21	48		
3.	Job Place of work How long?	Waiter Sunny Snack Bar 2 years	Engineer London 21 years		
4.	Home How long?	Middleford 1960	Applefield 1957		
5.	Married? How long?	No —	Yes 18 years		
6.	Children?	—	2		
7.	Car? How long?	Ford 3 Months	Renault 2 years		

Now read this paragraph:

John White is 21 years old. He is a waiter. He works at the Sunny Snack Bar. He has been a waiter for two years. His home is in Middleford; he has lived there since 1960. He is not married and he has no children. He has a Ford car; he has had it for three months.

Now write a paragraph about Jack Lester:

Jack Lester . . . .

. . . .

. . . .

. . . .

. . . .

Now write a paragraph about yourself:

I ....
....
....
....
....
....

Now write a paragraph about your friend:

....
....
....
....
....

Vocabulary

already	ɔːl'redi	....	Monday	'mʌndi	....
boss	bɔs	....	order (v.)	'ɔːdə*	....
call (n.)	kɔːl	....	outside	aut'said	....
chapter	'tʃæptə*	....	perfect	'pə'fikt	....
copy (n.)	'kɔpi	....	reader	'riːdə*	....
drill	dril	....	reference	'refərəns	....
fortnight	'fɔːtnait	....	section	'sekʃən	....
holiday	'hɔlidi	....	several	'sevrəl	....
homework	'houmwəːk	....	since	sins	....
January	'dʒænjuəri	....	speak	spiːk	....
knitting	'nitiŋ	....	special	'speʃl	....
language	'læŋgwidʒ	....	trouble	'trʌbl	....
magazine	mægə'ziːn	....	Wednesday	'wenzdi	....
matter	'mætə*	....	week	wiːk	....
mean (v.)	miːn	....	yet	jet	....
message	'mesidʒ	....			

12

Summary 13 Language Summary

1. Past Simple of BE
a) Affirmative

Notice: in these sentences WAS is pronounced /wəz/ and WERE is pronounced /wə*/.

I He She	was	in London at home on holiday	yesterday. last week.
You We They	were		

Put WAS or WERE in the spaces. Say the sentences first (remember the pronunciation), then write them.

a) Arthur and Mary . . . . at work yesterday.

b) Sheila . . . . ill last week.

c) John and I . . . . on holiday last week.

d) You and your brother . . . . in Paris last year.

e) The weather . . . . very bad yesterday.

f) The Newtons . . . . at church last Sunday.

b) Interrogative and Short Answers

In the questions WAS is pronounced either /wəz/ or /wɔz/ and WERE is pronounced either /wə*/ or /wə:*/. In the answer WAS is pronounced /wɔz/, WERE is pronounced /wə:*/, WASN'T is pronounced /wɔznt/ and WEREN'T is pronounced /wə:nt/.

Was	I he she	in London at home on holiday	yesterday? last week?	Yes,	I he she	was.	No,	I he she	wasn't.
Were	you we they				you we they	were.		you we they	weren't.

c) Negative

1)

I He She	wasn't	in London at home on holiday	yesterday. last week.
You We They	weren't		

2)

I He She	was	not	in London at home on holiday	yesterday. last week.
You We They	were			

Look at these two lists:

at work	yesterday
at school	last night
at home	last Sunday
at the cinema	last week
at the football match	
in the park	
in London	
on holiday	

Now practise these dialogues with a friend, using phrases from the lists:

a) Were you *at work yesterday?*
    Yes, I was/No, I wasn't. Were you?
  Yes, I was/ No, I wasn't.

b) Arthur wasn't *at work yesterday.*
    Why not? Was he ill?
  No, he wasn't ill. He was *in London.*

c) Mary and Sheila were *at work yesterday.*
    No, they weren't. They were *at home.*
  No, you're wrong. I'm sure they were *at work.*

d) Was Mr Steele *at work yesterday?*
    No, he wasn't.
  Where was he then?
    He was *at home.*

Look at Mr Steele's diary for last Sunday:

Sunday

Home all day; library closed. Wife also home, son and daughter in London. Morning — in garden; weather not good, lots of black clouds. Lunch good - two guests. Asleep all afternoon. A little rain in evening. Television not very interesting.

Now write a paragraph about Mr Steele, using only WAS *and* WERE *as the verbs:*

Last Sunday Mr Steele . . . .

. . . .

. . . .

. . . .

. . . .

Now write a paragraph about yourself last Sunday:

Last Sunday I . . . .

. . . .

. . . .

. . . .

2. Tail Questions
a) Type 1

We use this type of tail question when we want a real answer (*yes* or *no*). This is the intonation:

You like ↘coffee, ↗don't you? Arthur isn't a ↘student, ↗is he?

If we expect or hope for the answer *yes*, we use this form:

Affirmative	Negative interrogative
I'm coming with you,	aren't I?
He's going to lock up,	isn't he?
You've read this book,	haven't you?
We get our pay today,	don't we?
Arthur was in Applefield last weekend,	wasn't he?
You can help me,	can't you?
Mary must put out the new magazines,	mustn't she?

If we expect or hope for the answer *no*, we use this form:

Negative	Affirmative interrogative
Doctor, I'm not ill,	am I?
You aren't going to leave me here,	are you?
She hasn't given the fish to the cat,	has she?
Sheila doesn't work at the library,	does she?
They weren't on holiday yesterday,	were they?
He can't ask me to work on Sunday,	can he?
They mustn't take him to hospital,	must they?

Make sentences with tail questions for these situations (some of your sentences must be affirmative with a negative tail question, others must be negative with an affirmative tail question). Say them first, then write them. Remember that in this type of tail question your voice must go up *when you say the tail question.*

Examples You want to know if your friend has got a car. The answer is probably yes. You ask: *You've got a car, haven't you?*

You want to known if Mr Steele was at work yesterday. The answer is probably no. You ask: *Mr Steele wasn't at work yesterday, was he?*

a) You want to know if Sheila lives in Middleford. The answer is probably yes. You ask:

Sheila . . . .

b) You want to know if your friend can come to your party. You hope the answer is yes. You ask:

You . . . .

c) You want to know if it is raining. You hope the answer is no. You ask:

It . . . .

d) You want to know if your friend speaks French. The answer is probably no. You ask:

You . . . .

e) You want to know if Arthur has bought a car yet. The answer is probably no. You ask:

Arthur ....

b) Type 2

This type of tail question is not a real question; it is a statement in the form of a question; we are sure that we are right. This is the intonation:

It's a ↘lovely day, ↘isn't it? Arthur can't type ↘very well, ↘can he?

Here are some more examples:

You aren't English,	are you?
Bruce has got a gold watch,	hasn't he?
Arthur doesn't live with his parents,	does he?
Sheila was at Jennifer's party,	wasn't she?
You can't speak perfect English yet,	can you?
We must all work hard	mustn't we?

Make sentences with tail questions (some affirmative, others negative) for these situations. Your voice must go down *when you say this type of tail question.*

Example   You are sure that the cat has eaten the fish, so you say:

The cat has eaten the fish, has'nt it?

a) You are sure that Mr Lester has been an engineer for 21 years, so you say:

Mr Lester ....

b) You are sure your friend can't drive a bus, so you say:

You ....

c) You are sure that Dr Newton doesn't like parties, so you say:

Dr Newton ....

d) You are sure that you have made a mistake in this exercise, so you say:

I ....

e) You are sure that Mrs Harrison is cooking dinner, so you say:

Mrs Harrison ....

3. Ordinals

1st	first	fə:st	16th	sixteenth	'siks'ti:nθ
2nd	second	'sekənd	17th	seventeenth	'sevn'ti:nθ
3rd	third	θə:d	18th	eighteenth	'ei'ti:nθ
4th	fourth	fɔ:θ	19th	nineteenth	'nain'ti:nθ
5th	fifth	fifθ	20th	twentieth	'twentiiθ
6th	sixth	siksθ	21st	twenty-first	'twenti'fə:st
7th	seventh	'sevənθ	30th	thirtieth	'θə:tiiθ
8th	eighth	eitθ	40th	fortieth	'fɔ:tiiθ
9th	ninth	nainθ	50th	fiftieth	'fiftiiθ
10th	tenth	tenθ	60th	sixtieth	'sikstiiθ
11th	eleventh	i'levnθ	70th	seventieth	'sevntiiθ
12th	twelfth	twelfθ	80th	eightieth	'eitiiθ
13th	thirteenth	'θə:'ti:nθ	90th	ninetieth	'naintiiθ
14th	fourteenth	'fɔ:'ti:nθ	100th	hundredth	'hʌndrədθ
15th	fifteenth	'fif'ti:nθ	1000th	thousandth	'θauzənθ

Say and write these ordinals:

a) 22nd ....

b) 33rd ....

c) 41st ....

d) 44th ....

e) 53rd ....

f) 55th ....

g) 66th ....

h) 77th ....

i) 88th ....

j) 99th ....

Vocabulary

allow	ə'lau	....	June	dʒuːn	....
April	'eipril	....	lock	lɔk	....
as	əz; æz	....	March	mɑːtʃ	....
August	'ɔːgəst	....	month	mʌnθ	....
boat	bout	....	November	nou'vembə*	....
broke	brouk	....	off	ɔf	....
bye-bye	'bai'bai	....	pay (n.)	pei	....
catch	kætʃ	....	pay-day	'peidei	....
December	di'sembə*	....	picnic	'piknik	....
diary	'daiəri	....	river	'rivə*	....
different	'difrənt	....	salary	'sæləri	....
each	iːtʃ	....	side	said	....
end	end	....	success	sək'ses	....
expect	ik'spekt	....	Town Hall	'taun 'hɔːl	....
February	'februəri	....	Tuesday	'tjuːzdi	....
great	greit	....	was	wəz; wɔz	....
hell	hel	....	weather	'weðə*	....
hope	houp	....	were	wə*; wəː*	....
hurry (n.)	'hʌri	....	wet	wet	....
idea	ai'diə	....	would	wud	....
injury	'indʒəri	....	year	'jiə*	....
July	dʒu'lai	....	yesterday	'jestədi	....

Michael	'maikl

Spain	spein

Summary 14   Language Summary

1. PAST SIMPLE
(affirmative)
a) Strong (irregular) verbs

I You He She We They	bought some food rang Mary up went to London had dinner in a restaurant	yesterday. last week. three days ago.

b) Weak (regular) verbs

I You He She We They	opened the window locked the door washed the floor cooked the chicken	last night. this morning. a minute ago.

We use this tense for past actions whose time is given and for actions in a finished period of past time. This is different from the Present Perfect tense (see Summary 11).

Look at these time phrases:

yesterday	last night
the day before yesterday	last week
three days ago	last month
on Tuesday	last year

When you use a time phrase like these, you must use the Past Simple tense. Say and write these sentences, using a time phrase and a verb in the Past Simple tense:

a) Sheila and Mary . . . . to the cinema . . . .

b) Arthur . . . . a lot of postcards . . . .

c) Bruce . . . . Arthur £1 . . . .

d) Mrs Newton . . . . T.V. . . . ., but her

nusband . . . . to the radio.

e) Mary . . . . a new coat . . . .

f) Mrs Harrison . . . . the shopping . . . .

g) Mr Steele . . . . *A New History of Middleford* . . . .

h) The ambulance . . . . Bruce to hospital . . . .

Read this paragraph:
Every morning Mr Lester gets up at seven o'clock. First he makes a cup of tea and takes it to his wife in bed, then he gets dressed and has breakfast. He goes to work by train. He has lunch in a pub, works all afternoon and catches the 5.30 train home. He has a bath before dinner, and after dinner he falls asleep in front of the television. At ten o'clock he puts the cat out of the house, goes upstairs, gets into bed, writes his diary, switches off the light and goes to sleep.

Mr Lester did all these things yesterday too. Write the paragraph:

Yesterday Mr Lester . . . .

. . . .

. . . .

. . . .

. . . .

. . . .

. . . .

. . . .

. . . .

. . . .

Now write a paragraph about yourself yesterday:

Yesterday I . . . .

. . . .

. . . .

. . . .

. . . .

. . . .

. . . .

. . . .

. . . .

2. ONE/SOME/ANY as pronouns

a) ONE

These sandwiches are good. Would you like Bruce has got a car. Has Arthur got	one?

b) SOME

Notice: SOME as a pronoun is pronounced /sʌm/.

This wine is good. I'm going to drink Those biscuits are cheap. I've just bought	some.

c) ANY

Can you lend me some money? I haven't got Pass me the pickled onions. Arthur doesn't want	any.

d) as subject

ONE and SOME can also be the subject of a verb, as in these sentences:

One Some	of these books	is are	about the history of Middleford.

Look at these lists:

A	B
some money	a dictionary
some matches	an alarm clock
some records	a knife
some gloves	a handkerchief
some keys	a pair of jeans
some medicine	a newspaper
some paper	a map
some postcards	a pullover
some magazines	a torch
some history books	an umbrella

Now practise these questions and answers with a friend.

a) *Your friend says:*
    I've got .... here.
    using a phrase from one of the lists. If the phrase comes from list A, you say:
    Have you? I've got some too.
    If the phrase comes from list B, you say:
    Have you? I've got one too.

b) *Your friend says:*
    Can you lend me ....?
    using a phrase from one of the lists. If the phrase comes from list A, you say:
    No, I'm sorry. I haven't got any.
    If the phrase comes from list B, you say:
    No, I'm sorry. I haven't got one.

3. ENOUGH

Notice the position of ENOUGH. It is placed after adjectives:

		1	2	
This glass This coat This chair	isn't	big warm comfortable	enough.	Give me another one.

But in front of nouns:

	1	2	
We haven't got	enough	chairs. tables. beds.	Go and get another one.

You and a friend are giving a party. Ask your friend questions with ENOUGH, like this:

Wine?   *Have we got enough wine?*

Room/big?   *Is the room big enough?*

a) Sandwiches?.....................................

b) Beer?...

c) Ice-cream/cold?................................

d) Records? ....

e) Room/warm?...................................

f) Chairs/comfortable? ....

4. TOO

That cheese This tea This floor	is	too	expensive. hot. dirty.	I can't	buy it. drink it. clean it.

Now your party is over. It wasn't a success. Tell your friend what was wrong with it, like this:

Wine/cold.　*The wine was too cold.*

a) Beer/warm ....

b) Room/small ....

c) Records/old ....

d) Coffee/hot...

e) Chairs/uncomfortable. ....

f) The guests/thirsty ....

5. Phrasal verbs

Notice the position of OUT, UP *and* ON *in these sentences.*

Arthur took out his trousers. He hung up his suit. He switched on the radio. He rang up Mary.	OR	He took his trousers out. He hung his suit up. He switched the radio on. He rang Mary up.
	BUT ONLY	He took them out. He hung it up. He switched it on. He rang her up.

Vocabulary

appear	ə'piə*	....	pass	pɑːs	....
basket	'bɑːskit	....	pickled	pikld	....
borrow	'bɔrou	....	pleased	pliːzd	....
bridge	bridʒ	....	plenty	'plenti	....

cheese	tʃiːz	....	pour	pɔː*	....
chicken	'tʃikin	....	programme	'prougræm	....
chilly	'tʃili	....	pullover	'puluvə*	·:................
clear	kliə*	....	rest	rest	....
cloudy	'klaudi	....	row	rou	·:................
coloured	'kʌləd	....	sandwich	'sændwitʃ	....
daughter	'dɔːtə*	....	sharp	ʃaːp	....
difficult	'difikʌlt	....	shirt	ʃəːt	....
downstream	daun'striːm	....	shoe	ʃuː	....
drawer	drɔːə*	....	skirt	skəːt	....
enough	i'nʌf	....	sky	skai	....
far	faː*	....	sleeve	sliːv	....
film	film	....	steer	'stiə*	....
flour	'flauə*	....	suit	sjuːt	....
forecast	'fɔːkaːst	....	sunshine	'sʌnʃain	....
fruit	fruːt	....	suppose	sə'pouz	....
ham	hæm	....	teacher	'tiːtʃə*	....
hang	hæŋ	....	temperature	'tempritʃə*	....
hanger	'hæŋə*	....	tie (v.)	tai	....
high	hai	....	timetable	'taim,teibl	....
hire	'haiə*	....	tree	triː	....
island	'ailənd	....	uncomfortable	,ʌŋ'kʌmftəbl	....
let	'let	....	untidy	ʌn'taidi	....
mind	maind	....	upstream	ʌp'striːm	....
off-licence	'ɔf,laisns	....	wardrobe	'wɔːdroub	....
onion	'ʌnjən	....	wide	waid	....

Adams	'ædəmz

Summary 15 Language Summary

1. PAST SIMPLE
   a) Interrogative and Short Answers

Did	I you he she we they	buy any food go to London wash the floor cook the chicken	yesterday?

Yes,	I you he she we they	did.

No,	I you he she we they	didn't.

Ask four friends if they did these things last Sunday. Put a tick in the columns if they did them.

	1	2	3	4
stay in bed late have a big breakfast read the Sunday newspapers go to church visit friends drive into the country work in the garden wash the car write letters do any homework				

Now write down their answers. Use phrases like 'Two of my friends ....',
'All of them ....', 'None of them ....'.

Last Sunday ....

....

....

....

....

....

b) Negative 1)

I You He She We They	didn't	buy any food go to London wash the floor cook the chicken	yesterday.

2)

I You He She We They	did not	buy any food go to London wash the floor cook the chicken	yesterday.

Go back to the people you asked about last Sunday and check their answers. Say sentences like this:
    You didn't stay in bed late last Sunday, did you?
or
    You stayed in bed late last Sunday, didn't you?

Look again at the list and write down the things you *did and the things* you *didn't do last Sunday.*

Last Sunday I . . . .

. . . .

. . . .

. . . .

. . . .

. . . .

. . . .

. . . .

2. HAVE
a) In the meaning of *possess*

When HAVE means *own* or *possess*, it is not used in continuous tenses. It is formed like this:

	Affirmative	Negative	Interrogative
Present	have (got) has (got)	haven't got hasn't got	have . . . got? has . . . got?
Past	had	didn't have	did . . . have?

24

b) In the meaning of *do*, *make*, *eat* etc.

When HAVE means *do*, *make*, *eat* etc., it is used in all tenses, like this:

	Affirmative	Negative	Interrogative
Present Simple	have	don't have doesn't have	do ... have? does ... have?
Present Continuous	am having are having is having	'm not having aren't having isn't having	am ... having? are ... having? is ... having?
Present Perfect	have had has had	haven't had hasn't had	have ... had? has ... had?
Past Simple	had	didn't have	did ... have?

Use the verb HAVE *in these sentences in the correct tense and form.*

a) What time .... you .... breakfast yesterday?

At seven o'clock.

.... you always .... it at seven o'clock?

No. Today, for example, I .... it at eight o'clock.

b) How many sisters .... Arthur .... ?

He .... only one.

How many brothers?

He .... not .... any brothers.

c) How many English lessons .... you .... a week?

I usually .... four, but last week I .... five.

d) .... you .... lunch yet?

No, I .... not usually .... it until one o'clock.

e) .... Arthur .... a car?

No. He .... not .... a driving licence either.

f) What's Arthur doing? .... he .... a bath?

No, he .... not .... a bath. He .... a shave.

Vocabulary

accelerator	ək'selə,reitə*	....	lever	'li:və*	....
along	ə'lɒŋ	....	middle	'midl	....
angry	'æŋgri	....	mirror	'mirə*	....

25

anyway	'eniwei	....	neutral	'nju:trəl	....
appointment	ə'pɔintmənt	....	pedal	'pedl	....
badly	'bædli	....	pick	pik	....
belt	belt	....	press	pres	....
brake	breik	....	provisional	prə'viʒnl	....
brick	brik	....	pupil	'pju:pl	....
canoe	cə'nu:	....	refuse	ri'fju:z	....
clutch	klʌtʃ	....	remember	ri'membə*	....
completely	kəm'pli:tli	....	report	ri'pɔ:t	....
continue	kən'tinju:	....	reserve	ri'zə:v	....
control (n.)	kən'troul	....	reverse	ri'və:s	....
did	did	....	steering-column	'stiəriŋ ˌkɔləm	....
engine	'endʒin	....	steering-wheel	'stiəriŋ wi:l	....
flower	'flauə*	....	straight	streit	....
following	'fɔlouwiŋ	....	symphony	'simfəni	....
foot-brake	'futbreik	....	terrible	'teribl	....
forget	fə'get	....	tiny	'taini	....
gear	'giə*	....	war	wɔ:*	....
hand-brake	'hænbreik	....	Whatsername	'wɔtsəˌneim	....
indicator	'indiˌkeitə*	....	worry	'wʌri	....
instructor	in'strʌktə*	....	whisky	'wiski	....
left	left	....			

Beethoven	'beithouvn
Elsie	'elsi
John	dʒɔn
Margaret	'mɑ:grət
Taylor	'teilə*

Blue Parrot	'blu: 'pærət
Coca Cola	'koukə 'koulə
Red Dragon	'red 'drægən

Summary 16 Language Summary

1. MAY

a) in the meaning of *possibility*

In this meaning MAY is used in the affirmative:

I It She	may	go out tonight or I rain tomorrow or it buy a new dress or she	may	stay at home. be fine. buy a new coat.

and in the negative:

You We They	may not	have enough money to buy a car. arrive until late. come to the party tomorrow.

but not in the interrogative.

It's three o'clock in the afternoon. Here are two lists of things you can do tonight:

A	B
go to the cinema	stay at home
listen to some Beethoven	watch TV
have dinner at home	eat at the Blue Parrot
do some homework	read a magazine
have a party	go to bed early

Now practise this dialogue with a friend, using phrases from the lists:
What are you going to do tonight?
I don't know. I may . . . . . .(list A). . . . , . or I may . . . . . .(list B). . . . . . .
Yes, I may . . . . . .(listB). . . . . . too.

Look at these two lists:

A	B
go to work	stay at home
write any postcards	put books on the shelves
have lunch at the Snack Bar	go to the Red Dragon
buy a new car	get a second-hand one
sleep at Mrs Harrison's	go home to Applefield

Now practise this dialogue with a friend:
Arthur may not . . . . . . (list A) . . . . . . tomorrow.
Why not?
Well, he may . . . . . . (list B) . . . . . . instead.

b) in the meaning of *permission*

May	I we	open the window, smoke, get a glass of water, help you,	please?

Yes, you may. No, you may not.

CAN is often used instead of MAY in this meaning.

Say and write questions starting 'May I . . . . . .' for these situations:

a) You have lost your dictionary. Your friend has got one. You ask:

. . . .

b) Your friend is reading but you want to hear the news on the radio. You ask:

. . . .

c) You want to buy a new watch. There is a nice one in the shop window. You go into the shop and ask: ....

....

d) Now you want to buy the watch. You have no money in your pocket, but you have a cheque-book. You ask: ....

e) You are in a snack bar. There isn't enough sugar in your coffee. You ask the waiter: ....

2. NEED in the meaning of *require*

In this meaning NEED is a normal verb.

	Affirmative	Interrogative	Negative
Present & Future	need needs	do ... need? does ... need?	don't need doesn't need
Past	needed	did ... need?	didn't need

Use NEED *in the correct tense and form in these sentences:*

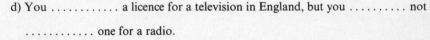

a) Mary's doing a difficult job. .... she .... any help?

b) There's been an accident. We .... an ambulance.

c) Was it cold in the park? .... you .... an overcoat?

d) You .... a licence for a television in England, but you .... not .... one for a radio.

e) I carried the oranges in my pockets, so I .... not .... a bag.

f) She isn't ill; she .... not .... any medicine.

g) .... you .... me, or may I go home now?

h) Michael .... a picnic basket for the picnic, so he borrowed one from his mother.

i) Arthur is broke again; he .... a bigger salary.

3. Expressions of time with 's

Normally 's is used as the possessive case for people:

> The boy's book
> Bruce's car

But it is also used in some expressions of time:

> This week's bargain
> Yesterday's newspaper
> Tomorrow's weather
> Next year's holiday
> Last week's television programmes

Vocabulary

alone	əˈloun	....	mileage	ˈmailidʒ	....
bargain (n.)	ˈbɑːgn	....	monthly	ˈmʌnθli	....
belong	biˈlɔŋ	....	motor	ˈmoutə*	....
block	blɔk	....	need	niːd	....
bright	brait	....	owner	ˈounə*	....
camera	ˈkæmrə	....	paint (n.)	peint	
cheque-book	ˈtʃek buk	....	pass	pɑːs	....
chocolate	ˈtʃɔklət	....	personally	ˈpəːsnəli	
close (v.)	klouz	....	police station	pəˈliːs ˌsteiʃn	
congratulations	kəŋˌgrætjuˈleiʃnz	....	price	prais	
cookery book	ˈkukri buk	....	question	ˈkwestʃn	....
deposit (n.)	diˈpɔzit	....	rid	rid	
difficulty	ˈdifiklti	....	road tax	ˈroud tæks	
else	els	....	salesman	ˈseilzmən	....
extra	ˈekstrə	....	scruffy	ˈskrʌfi	....
grammar	ˈgræmə*	....	second-hand	ˈseknd ˌhænd	
heap	hiːp	....	seem	siːm	....
information	ˌinfəˈmeiʃn	....	shiny	ˈʃaini	....
inside	inˈsaid	....	showroom	ˈʃourum	
instalment	ˌinˈstɔːlmənt	....	sports car	ˈspɔːts kɑː*	
junk	djʌŋk	....	suitable	ˈsjuːtəbl	
low	lou	....	taste (v.)	teist	....
luck	lʌk	....	tenner	ˈtenə*	
main	mein	....	test	test	....
mart	mɑːt	....	used	juːzd	
may	mei	....	windscreen	ˈwindskriːn	....
mechanic	məˈkænik	....	yellow	ˈjelou	

Charlie	ˈtʃɑːli	

Summary 17 Language Summary

1. WILL/SHALL Future
  a) Affirmative

1)

I'll We'll You'll He'll She'll They'll	clean the car go to the bank drive to Applefield take Sheila to the seaside	this afternoon. tomorrow. next week.

2)

I We	shall will	clean the car go to the bank drive to Applefield take Sheila to the seaside	this afternoon. tomorrow. next week.
You He She They	will		

Fill the spaces with a verb in the WILL/SHALL *future tense. Say the sentences first (use* 'LL*), then write them (use* WILL *or* SHALL*).*

a) My train leaves in half an hour.

O.K., I .... you to the station in my car.

b) Some new books have arrived, Mary.

Don't worry, Mr Steele. Arthur .... them on the shelves

this afternoon.

c) You forgot to write to your uncle.

Never mind. I've got his telephone number, I .... him

tomorrow morning.

d) It's Sheila's birthday tomorrow.

Is it? Right, we .... her a cake.

e) It's hot in here.

All right, I .... the window.

f) How is he going to get to London? He hasn't got a car.

No, but he .... probably .... one.

g) We need some flowers for this room.

Perhaps Mrs Newton .... some from her garden this

afternoon.

h) This wine is excellent.

Good, I . . . . you some more.

i) Look at all this homework!

Yes, there's a lot. I'm busy tonight, but perhaps I . . . . it

at the weekend.

j) They aren't going to drive to Sheffield without stopping, are they?

No, they . . . . probably . . . . for a meal in Nottingham.

b) Interrogative and Short Answers

Ask and answer these questions:

Will	you he she they	clean the car go to the bank drive to Applefield take Sheila to the seaside	this afternoon? tomorrow? next week?

Yes,	I we	shall. will.	No,	I we	shan't. won't.
	you he she they	will.		you he she they	won't.

c) Negative

Say the sentences in table 1), read the sentences in table 2).

1)

I We	shan't won't	clean the car go to the bank drive to Applefield take Sheila to the seaside	this afternoon. tomorrow. next week.
You He She They	won't		

2)

I We	shall will	not	clean the car go to the bank drive to Applefield take Sheila to the seaside	this afternoon. tomorrow. next week.
You He She They	will			

Ask and answer questions beginning 'Will . . . . . .' about these pictures, as in the example. (Notice the position of 'probably' in the answer.)

Will Arthur take Mary
to the party, do you think?
No, he probably won't.

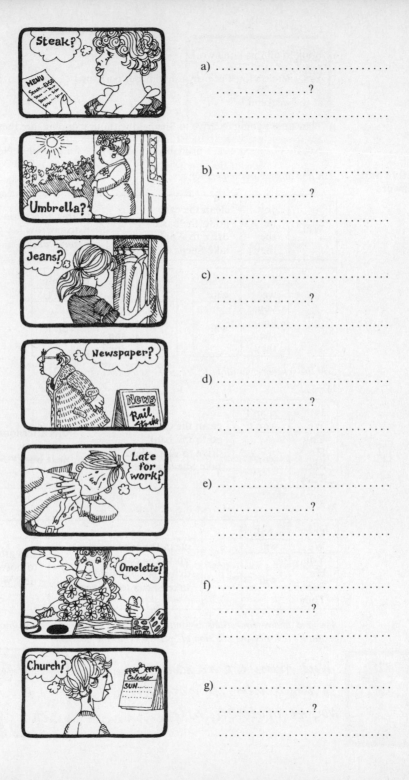

a) ....
........................?
....

b) ....
........................?
....

c) ....
........................?
....

d) ....
........................?
....

e) ....
........................?
....

f) ....
........................?
....

g) ....
........................?
....

h) . . . .

. . . . ?

. . . .

2. SHALL I . . . ?

This form is used as a request to know someone's wishes.

Shall I	clean the windscreen check the tyres fill up the radiator check the battery put the petrol in	for you?	Yes, please. That's very kind of you. No, never mind.

You and a friend have got to clean the house tomorrow. Read these lists of things you have got to do.

A	B
wash the kitchen floor	wash the bathroom floor
wash the milk bottles	throw away the beer bottles
clean the inside windows	clean the outside windows
wash the clothes	do the ironing
tidy the sitting-room	tidy the bedrooms
do the cooking	do the washing up

Now practise this dialogue with your friend, using phrases from the lists:

Shall I . . . . . . (*list A*) . . . . . . ?

No, I'll . . . . . . (*list A*) . . . . . . Will you . . . . . . (*list B*) . . . . . . ?

O.K.

3. SHALL WE . . . ? LET'S . . .

Both these forms are used to make suggestions. This is the question:

What shall we do	tonight? tomorrow? at the weekend?

This is the answer:

Shall we	go to the cinema? watch television? drive to the seaside?	OR	Let's	go to the cinema. watch television. drive to the seaside.

Practise this dialogue with a friend, using 'Shall we . . . . . . ?' *or* 'Let's . . . . . .'

FRIEND: What shall we do on Sunday?

YOU: . . . .

FRIEND: No, we did that *last* Sunday. Suggest something different.

YOU: . . . .

FRIEND: That's not a very good idea. Try another suggestion.

YOU: . . . .

33

FRIEND: No, still not good enough. Try again.

YOU: ....

FRIEND: That's a bit better. But I think we did *that* last Sunday too. Any other suggestions?

YOU: ....

FRIEND: O.K., we'll do that.

4. NEED

In this meaning NEED is only used in the negative and interrogative patterns. In the negative the meaning is absence of obligation:

Present & Future	I You They	needn't	go to work tomorrow; it's Sunday. hurry; it's still early. go by car; there are plenty of buses.

Past	I You They	didn't need to	go to work yesterday; it was Sunday. hurry; it was still early. go by car; there were plenty of buses.

Fill the spaces with a negative form of NEED *and a verb.*

a) Dr Newton has plenty of money, so he .... to the bank.

b) Arthur .... Mrs Harrison any money until next month.

c) The student already knew the words, so he .... them.

e) If this question is too difficult for you, you .... it.

e) There were plenty of porters, so she .... her suitcases.

f) This car goes fast, so you .... the accelerator pedal very hard.

g) I had a map, so I .... the way.

h) There's a lift in this building, so you .... the stairs.

In the interrogative the meaning is very similar to MUST.

Present & Future	Need	I you they	go to work tomorrow? hurry? go by car?		Yes, No,	I you they	must. needn't.

Past	Did	I you they	need to	go to work yesterday? hurry? go by car?		Yes, No,	I you they	did. didn't.

Vocabulary

airport	'ɛəpɔːt	....	petrol	'petrl	....
area	'ɛəriə	....	petrol gauge	'petrl ˌgeidʒ	....
bank	bæŋk	....	pity	'piti	....
battery	'bætəri	....	pork	pɔːk	....
beef	biːf	....	radiator	'reidieitə*	....
bicycle	'baisikl	....	raincoat	'reiŋkout	....
castle	'kɑːsl	....	rate	reit	....
centigrade	'sentigreid	....	ride	raid	....
count	kaunt	....	sake	seik	....
die	dai	....	sensible	'sensibl	....
distilled	dis'tild	....	shall	ʃæl; ʃəl	....
dry	drai	....	shan't	ʃɑːnt	....
enjoy	in'dʒɔi	....	ship	ʃip	....
everywhere	'evriwɛə*	....	square	skwɛə*	....
family	'fæmili	....	stamp (n.)	stæmp	....
fantastic	fæn'tæstik	....	stop (v.)	stɔp	....
fill	fil	....	sunglasses	'sʌnˌglɑːsiz	....
gallon	'gæln	....	sunny	'sʌni	....
glad	glæd	....	surprised	sə'praizd	....
hill	hil	....	tyre	'taiə*	....
idiot	'idiət	....	wake	weik	....
lemonade	ˌlemə'neid	....	will	wil	....
lighter	'laitə*	....	wonder	wʌndə*	....
line	lain	....	won't	wount	....
magnificent	mæg'nifisnt	....	wreck	rek	....
midnight	'midnait	....	zoo	zuː	....
museum	mjuː'ziəm	....			
navigate	'nævigeit	....			
park	pɑːk	....			

Corfe	kɔːf
Swanage	'swɔnidʒ
Weymouth	'weiməθ

Summary 18 Language Summary

1. **Comparison of Adjectives and Adverbs**

a) One-syllable adjectives and adverbs

	Comparative	Superlative
small	smaller	smallest
large	larger	largest
fast	faster	fastest
poor	poorer	poorest

b) One-syllable adjectives ending in vowel + 't', 'g', 'd' or 'n'

big	bigger	biggest
fat	fatter	fattest
thin	thinner	thinnest

hot

c) Two-syllable adjectives and adverbs ending in 'y' or 'er'

pretty	prettier	prettiest
clever	cleverer	cleverest
early	earlier	earliest

d) Other adjectives and adverbs of two or more syllables

intelligent	more intelligent	most intelligent
careful	more careful	most careful
miserable	more miserable	most miserable
intelligently	more intelligently	most intelligently

e) Irregular adjectives and adverbs

good	better	best
well	better	best
bad	worse	worst
badly	worse	worst
much	more	most
many	more	most
little	less	least
far	{ farther { further	{ farthest { furthest

Say and write the comparative and superlative of these adjectives:

busy ..busier..than.. ....

difficult .More..diff....than ....

dry .dryer....than ....

hard ...harder..than ....

interesting ...More...inter...than ....

sad ...sadder...... ....

slow ...slower..than ....

wet ...wetter...than ....

36

Fill the spaces with ONE word.

a) Arthur's car is .... scruffiest car .... Middleford.

b) Dr Newton's house is bigger .... Mr Steele's.

c) *Darling Mary* ran faster .... *Bright Thursday*.

d) This is the .... interesting book .... the library.

e) It's warmer today .... it was yesterday.

f) Arthur's room is always untidy, but today it is .... untidy .... ever.

g) *Mark Time* was .... slowest horse in the race.

2. ONE/ONES

Adjectives of quality can be used with the pronouns ONE and ONES (see Summary 14 for ONE used as the object or subject of a verb).

Mary has a red dress but Sheila has a green Arthur wanted a new car but he bought an old This table is too small. I need a bigger	one.

These apples are too expensive. Give me some cheaper It's easier to teach intelligent students than stupid Mrs Harrison's clothes are ugly but Mary's got some very pretty	ones.

Practise this situation with two friends. You are buying some new things for your flat or house. First read these lists:

table	long
armchair	comfortable
bed	wide
light	attractive
cupboard	large
bath	fantastic
television	cheap
stove	suitable
radio	unusual
fridge	big

One of your friends is the salesman. He says things like:
This table is quite long.
using words from the lists. Your other friend says:
That one over there looks longer.
And you say:
I think this one here is the longest one of all.

3. EVER
a) in questions

Practise these questions and answers with a friend:

Have you	ever	been to the races? bet on a horse? won any money?	Yes, several times. No, never.
Do you		go to the races? bet on horses? win any money?	Yes, often. No, never.

37

b) with superlatives

It's the slowest horse I've		seen
He's the most intelligent man I've		known
It's the best meal I've	ever	eaten
It's the fastest car I've		driven
She's the prettiest girl I've		met

Look again at the two lists in 2) and say sentences with 'ever'. e.g.
That's the longest table I've ever seen.

4. Questions with end prepositions

1	2	3
What	are you looking	at?
Who	did Arthur go to the races	with?
Which	horse will you put your money	on?
Who	is she talking	to?
Where	are they going	(to)?
What	are you thinking	about?

Fill the spaces with a preposition.

a) Who does that house belong . . . . ?

b) Who did you borrow that book . . . . ?

c) Which programme did you listen . . . . ?

d) What is Arthur dreaming . . . . ?

e) Who are you waiting . . . . ?

f) Which bed will you sleep . . . . ?

g) Who will you give that present . . . . ?

h) Which platform does the train leave . . . . ?

i) Who did he lend his car . . . . ?

Vocabulary

apple	'æpl	. . . .	least	li:st	. . . .
attractive	ə'træktiv	. . . .	less	les	. . . .
best	best	. . . .	life	laif	. . . .
bet	bet	. . . .	meeting	'mi:tiŋ	. . . .
better	'betə*	. . . .	more	mɔ:*	. . . .
clever	'klevə*	. . . .	necessary	'nesisri	. . . .
collect	kə'lekt	. . . .	never	'nevə*	. . . .

condition	kən'diʃn	....	pleasant	'pleznt	....
darling	'dɑːliŋ	....	race	reis	....
decide	di'said	....	race card	'reis kɑːd	....
double	'dʌbl	....	reason	'riːzn	....
duty	'djuːti	....	rude	ruːd	....
edge	edʒ	....	smooth	smuːð	....
face	feis	....	tall	tɔːl	....
farther	'fɑːðə*	....	teeth	tiːθ	....
favourite	'feivrit	....	than	ðæn	....
finally	'fainəli	....	tooth	tuːθ	....
further	'fəːðə*	....	traffic	'træfik	....
grey	grei	....	trip	trip	....
heavy	'hevi	....	unpleasant	ʌn'pleznt	....
horse	hɔːs	....	usual	'juːʒuəl	....
however	hau'evə*	....	while	wail	....
illegal	i'liːgl	....	win	win	....
intelligent	in'telidʒnt	....	worn	wɔːn	....
Italian	i'tæliən	....	worse	wəːs	....
jockey	'dʒɔki	....	worst	wəːst	....

Fiat	'fiːət
Mark Time	'mɑːk 'taim
Volkswagen	'vɔːkswɑːgn

Fetlock Park	ˌfetlɔk 'pɑːk
Paris	'pæris
Salisbury	'sɔlzbri

Summary 19 Language Summary

1. Impersonal YOU

What do		write with?		You	write with a pen.
How do	you	learn to drive?			go to a driving school.
Where can		buy whisky?			can buy it at the off-licence.

Read again the text and dialogue of Chapter 15 and the beginning of Chapter 16. Then write a paragraph about how you learn to drive in England, using the impersonal YOU. *Here are some notes to help you:*

First, provisional licence; then, driving school; appointment for lesson; learn about controls; when/know about gears, clutch, brake, accelerator, start driving; after many lessons, driving test; then, driving licence; then, a car.

First, ...

. . . .

. . . .

. . . .

. . . .

. . . .

2. Conditionals
   a) 'General' conditions

	Present tense	Present tense
If	you eat too much,	you get fat.
	the sun shines,	it's warm.
	you put £1 on a horse at 10–1,	you win £20.

Notice: in this sort of conditional you can say WHEN instead of IF. You can also put the IF part of the sentence at the end:

You get fat if you eat too much.

Write out these questions in full, using the impersonal YOU *and an* IF *clause. Then answer the questions.*

Example   Where/go/if/want/borrow books?

Where do you go if you want to borrow books?
You go to a library.

a) What/buy/if/want/send a letter?

What . . . .

You . . . .

b) How many eggs/need/if/want/make an omelette?

How many eggs . . . .

You . . . .

c) How much/win/if/put £10/horse at 5–1?

How much . . . .

You . . . .

d) What language/must/learn/if/want/work in Italy?

What language . . . .

You . . . .

e) How many people/need/if/want/play football?

How many people . . . .

You . . . .

f) What/wear/if/go swimming? . . . .

What . . . .

You . . . .

b) 'Possible' conditions

		Present tense	Future tense
If		it rains, Middleford wins, you work hard,	I'll go to the cinema. Michael will be glad. you'll pass the test.

Notice: in this sort of conditional you cannot say WHEN instead of IF. But you can put the IF part of the sentence at the end.

> I'll go to the cinema if it rains.

Write out these sentences, putting the verbs into the correct tense:

a) If you (BE) late for school again, I (BE) very angry.

. . . .

b) If he (NOT ARRIVE) this evening, perhaps he (ARRIVE) tomorrow morning.

. . . .

. . . .

c) What his supporters (SAY) if Fred (NOT SCORE) a goal next Saturday?

. . . .

. . . .

d) If I (COOK) the lunch, you (WASH) the plates?

. . . .

e) If you (LEAVE) the car here, the police (TAKE) it away.

. . . .

f) I (TELEPHONE) you immediately if I (HEAR) any news.

. . . .

Practise this dialogue with a friend:
Will you play football tomorrow?
   Only if it's fine.
And if it isn't fine?
   I'll watch T.V.
Now practise the same dialogue, using these phrases:

a) you/go to the party?
   I/get an invitation.
   you/(not) get an invitation?
   I/stay at home.
b) Middleford/win the match?
   Fred/play well.
   Fred/(not) play well?
   Didcot/win.
c) Didcot/kick off?
   their captain/win the toss.
   he/(not) win the toss?
   Middleford/kick off.

d) Arthur and Jennifer/visit the castle?
   they/have enough time.
   they/(not) have enough time?
   they/(not) visit it.
e) Mr Steele/go to France for his holiday?
   he/have enough money.
   he/(not) have enough money?
   he/go to Bournemouth.
f) you/lend me some money?
   you/give it back soon.
   I/(not) give it back?
   I/be very angry.

3. Infinitive of Purpose

Why	did Michael come into the library? did Arthur go to the Car Mart? do you come to these lessons?	To	borrow a book. buy a car. learn English.

Put an infinitive of purpose into these sentences:

Example   Mrs Harrison went to the butcher's *to buy* some meat.

a) After dinner he sat down . . . . a letter.

b) She stood up . . . . her coat.

c) They walked down to the river . . . . a boat for the afternoon.

d) I'm going upstairs . . . . a bath.

e) He got out of bed . . . . the light.

f) He took the key out of his pocket . . . . the door.

g) She ran fast . . . . the bus.

h) She went into the kitchen . . . . a cup of tea.

Vocabulary

accept	ək'sept	. . . .	loud	laud	. . . .
against	ə'genst	. . . .	lucky	'lʌki	. . . .
association	ə'sousi'eiʃn	. . . .	match	mætʃ	. . . .
beard	biəd	. . . .	mate	meit	. . . .

42

bottom	'bɔtəm	. . . .	odds	ɔdz	. . . .
building	'bildiŋ	. . . .	original	ə'ridʒənl	. . . .
captain	'kæptin	. . . .	part	pɑ:t	. . . .
centre forward	ˌsentə 'fɔ:wəd	. . . .	player	'pleiə*	. . . .
chap	tʃæp	. . . .	racquet	'rækit	. . . .
club	klʌb	. . . .	razor	'reizə*	. . . .
crowded	'kraudid	. . . .	referee	ˌrefə'ri:	. . . .
deliberate	di'librit	. . . .	rich	ritʃ	. . . .
deliberately	di'libritli	. . . .	roll	roul	
derby	'dɑ:bi	. . . .	rugby	'rʌgbi	
division	di'viʒn	. . . .	rugger	'rʌgə*	
during	'djuəriŋ	. . . .	scarf	skɑ:f	. . . .
foul	faul	. . . .	scarves	skɑ:vz	. . . .
goal	goul	. . . .	score	skɔ:*	. . . .
ground	graund	. . . .	season	'si:zn	. . . .
happen	'hæpən	. . . .	shorts	ʃɔ:ts	. . . .
hero	'hiərou	. . . .	sign	sain	. . . .
if	if		soccer	'sɔkə*	. . . .
imagine	i'mædʒin	. . . .	spare	spɛə*	. . . .
invitation	ˌinvi'teiʃn	. . . .	sportsman	'spɔ:tsmən	. . . .
keen	ki:n	. . . .	stand (n.)	stænd	. . . .
kick	kik	. . . .	supporter	sə'pɔ:tə*	. . . .
kick-off	'kikɔf	. . . .	toss	tɔs	. . . .
kind	kaind	. . . .	turnstile	'tə:nstail	. . . .
league	li:g	. . . .	unpopular	ʌn'pɔpjulə*	. . . .

Didcot United	'didkət ju:'naitid		
Fred Merton	'fred 'mə:tən	China	'tʃainə
Middleford	'midlfəd	Mt. Everest	ˌmaunt 'evərist
Rangers	'reindʒəz	The South Pole	ðə 'sauθ 'poul
Neasden Rovers	'ni:sdən 'rouvəz		

Summary 20 Language Summary

1. PAST CONTINUOUS
  a) Affirmative

See Summary 13 for the pronunciation of WAS, WERE, WASN'T and WEREN'T.

I He She	was	watching television. working.
You We They	were	listening to the radio. sleeping.
It	was	raining.

We use this tense for actions which began in the past and continued in the past; we do not know when they began or when they ended:

> At eight o'clock yesterday evening I was watching television.

We use the Past Simple for actions at a definite time in the past:

> At seven o'clock yesterday evening I switched on the television.

Say and write what these people were doing *at eight o'clock last night and what they* did *ten minutes later, as in the example.*

At eight o'clock last night, Arthur was filling in his pools coupon. Ten minutes later he put it in his overcoat pocket.

a) ....
....
....

b) ....
....
....

c) ....
....
....

44

d) ....

....

....

e) ....

....

....

f) ....

....

....

What were you doing at eight o'clock last night? Write it down:

....

....

We often use the Past Simple and the Past Continuous tenses together:

I was watching television He was working They were listening to the radio	when	the telephone rang. Mr Steele came in. someone rang the bell.

Put the verbs in brackets into the Past Simple or the Past Continuous tense:

a) Bruce (PAY) .... the bill while Mary (PUT) ....
.... her coat on.

b) When she (WASH) .... her skirt, she (FIND) ....
a pound note in the pocket.

c) I (SEE) .... Arthur in the street yesterday, but he (RUN) ......
.... for a bus and (NOT HAVE) .... time to
speak to me.

d) When Jennifer (GET) .... home, her parents (HAVE) ....
.... dinner.

e) My car (BREAK DOWN) .... yesterday while I (DRIVE) ....
.... to work.

45

f) When she (OPEN) .... the door, a man (STAND) ....
.... on the doorstep. It (BE) .... her
uncle, but she (NOT RECOGNIZE) .... him
because he (WEAR) .... dark glasses.

g) The man (GET OFF) .... the bus without paying while the
conductor (COLLECT) .... fares upstairs.

h) The film (START) .... while we (BUY) ....
the tickets, so we (NOT SEE) .... the first few minutes.

b) Interrogative and Short Answers

Was	I he she	watching television? working?
Were	you we they	listening to the radio? sleeping?
Was	it	raining?

Yes,	I he she	was.
	you we they	were.
	it	was.

No,	I he she	wasn't.
	you we they	weren't.
	it	wasn't.

c) Negative

I He She	wasn't	watching television. working.
You We They	weren't	listening to the radio. sleeping.
It	wasn't	raining.

I He She	was		watching television. working.
You We They	were	not	listening to the radio. sleeping.
It	was		raining.

Read these lists:

A	B
wash the car	sit in an armchair
work in the garden	listen to the radio
paint the kitchen	watch television
do the washing up	read the newspaper
clean the windows	look at some magazines

Now practise these dialogues with a friend, using phrases from the lists:

a) John came round to see me yesterday.
　　Did he? What were you doing?
　I was .... *(list A)* ....
　　Did he help you?
　No! He just ....*(list B)* ....

b) Did Peter .... *(list A)* .... yesterday?
　　I don't know. He certainly wasn't .... *(list A)* .... when I
　　went round to see him.
　What *was* he doing?
　　He wasn't doing anything really. He was just .... *(list B)* ....

2. HAVE TO

a) Affirmative

In the affirmative HAVE TO means almost the same as MUST. But there is no past tense of MUST.

I must go now.	OR	I have to go now.
I must go tomorrow.	OR	I'll have to go tomorrow.
		I had to go yesterday.

b) Interrogative

In the interrogative HAVE TO means almost the same as MUST or NEED. But again there is no past tense of MUST.

Must I go now?	OR	Need I go now?	OR	Do I have to go now?
Must I go tomorrow	OR	Need I go tomorrow?	OR	Shall/will I have to go tomorrow?
		Did I need to go yesterday?	OR	Did I have to go yesterday?

c) Negative

In the negative HAVE TO means almost the same as NEED.

I needn't go now.	OR	I don't have to go now.
I needn't go tomorrow.	OR	I shan't/won't have to go tomorrow.
I didn't need to go yesterday.	OR	I didn't have to go yesterday.

Use HAVE TO *in the correct tense in these sentences:*

a) I'm sorry I was late for work yesterday. I . . . . go to the dentist's.

b) You . . . . not . . . . decide immediately, but you . . . . decide before next week.

c) He usually starts work at 8.30, so he . . . . leave home at 7.30.

d) There was plenty of time; we . . . . not . . . . hurry.

e) The banks are closed today; we . . . . wait until tomorrow for our money.

f) 'The police took my car away last week.' '. . . . . you . . . . collect it from the police station?'

g) . . . . I . . . . make an appointment to see the doctor?' 'No, you . . . . not . . . . make an appointment, but you . . . . wait for at least an hour.'

h) Mary . . . . not . . . . put the new books on the shelves. Arthur will do it.

i) I cut my hand badly and . . . . , put a bandage on it.

j) I want to buy this car by instalments. How much deposit . . . . I . . . . pay?

47

Vocabulary

absolutely	ˌæbsəˈluːtli	....	mad	mæd	....
apologize	əˈpɔlədʒaiz	....	nil	nil	
brief	briːf	....	nonsense	ˈnɔnsəns	....
celebrate	ˈselibreit	....	notice	ˈnoutis	....
coupon	ˈkuːpɔn	....	oil	ɔil	....
draw (n.)	drɔː	....	pools	puːlz	....
envelope	ˈenviloup	....	postman	ˈpousmən	....
excited	ikˈsaitid	....	receive	riˈsiːv	....
furious	ˈfjuəriəs	....	result	riˈzʌlt	....
haircut	ˈhɛəkʌt	....	Scottish	ˈskɔtiʃ	
interest	ˈintrist	....	transistor	trɑːnˈsistə*	....
joy	dʒɔi	....	turn	təːn	....
lose	luːz	....	understand	ˌʌndəˈstænd	....

Ayr	ɛə*	Hearts	hɑːts
Brentford	ˈbrentfəd	Hibernian	hiˈbəːniən
Bury	ˈberi	Morton	ˈmɔːtən
Celtic	ˈseltik	Motherwell	ˈmʌðəwel
Chester	ˈtʃestə*	Northampton	nɔːˈθæmptən
Colchester	ˈkoultʃistə*	Partick Thistle	ˈpɑːtik ˈθisl
Dundee	dʌnˈdiː	Scunthorpe	ˈskʌnθɔːp
East Fife	ˈiːst ˈfaif		